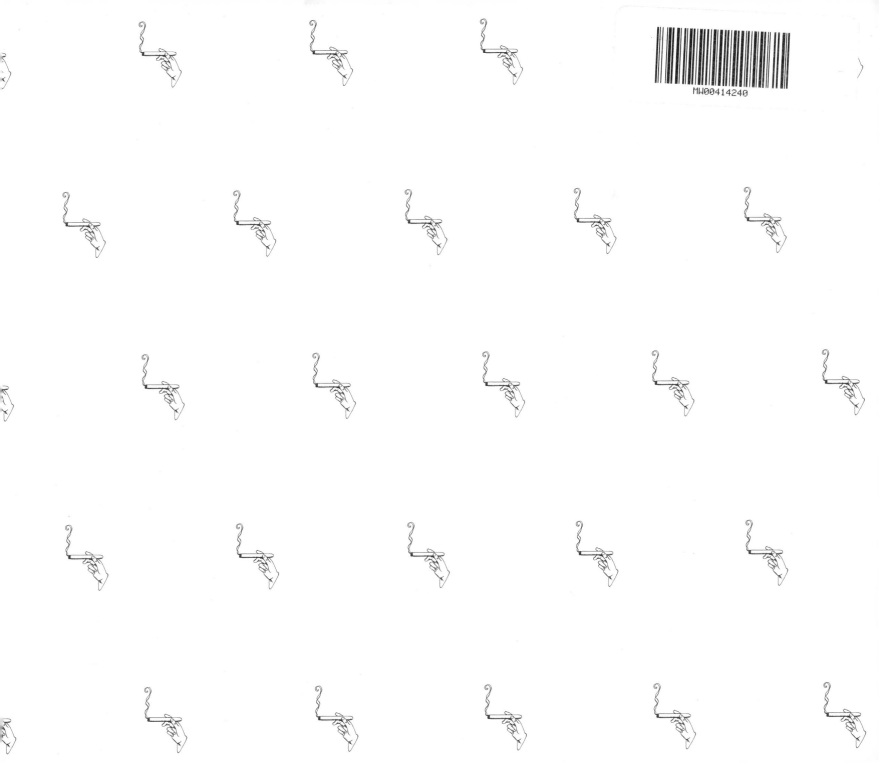

The Handmade Cigar

Collector's Guide & Journal

The Handmade Cigar
Collector's Guide & Journal

Written and Produced by Tom Connor & Jim Downey

CollinsPublishers
A Division of HarperCollinsPublishers

Collins books may be purchased for educational, business or sales promotional use. For information please write: Special Markets Department, HarperCollins Publishers, Inc., 10 East 53rd Street, New York, NY 10022.

FIRST EDITION

Designed by Laura Campbell
Cover design & art by Gerard Huerta

All photographs copyright © 1997 by J. Barry O'Rourke except: Henry Clay, Marlene Dietrich, Ernest Hemingway, Warren Harding, Rudyard Kipling, George Sand, W.C. Fields, Milton Berle and Jackie Gleason courtesy of the New York Public Library; Winston Churchill, John F. Kennedy, Ulysses S. Grant, Fidel Castro, Al Capone, Sigmund Freud, Samuel Clemens, Evelyn Waugh, Groucho Marx and Ernie Kovacs from Archive Photos; Virgina Woolf, Clarence Darrow, H.L. Mencken, John Quincy Adams and the Duke of Windsor from Culver Pictures, Inc.; Babe Ruth and Alfred Hitchcock from Bettmann Archives.

ISBN 0-00-649169-3

Printed in Hong Kong

97 98 99 00 01 ❖/HK 10 9 8 7 6 5 4 3 2 1

Acknowledgments

Many people have contributed their time, cigars and expertise to this book. We are indebted to Benjamin Menendez, Alfonse Mayer, Edgar Cullman, Sr., and Maribeth Schneider of the General Cigar Company; to Don Carlos Fuente, Carlos Fuente, Jr., and master roller Luis Rosario of A. Fuente y Cia; and to Christoph Kull, Edward Sahakian, Hendrik Kelner and Susan Coward of Davidoff of Geneva. Great appreciation goes to Shelly Jacobs in Minneapolis; Graves "Smitty" Smith of Nat Sherman's Fifth Avenue store in New York City; and Tom Hinds of Thomas Hinds Tobacconist in Toronto. Special thanks are due to Robert Telli; John O'Hearn; Jack Rapoport, Esq.; Stephen Curtis; Robert Ward; Jeff Kaminsky; Steve Swanson; Richard DiMeola of the Consolidated Cigar Company; Jorge Padrón of the Padrón Cigar Company in Miami; Ernesto Perez-Carrillo of El Credito Cigar Company in Miami; Lew Rothman of JR Tobacco; and to Desmond Sautter of Sautter of Mayfield and Simon Chase of Hunters & Frankau in London. Thanks also to Catherine St. John and Joe Lentine of Owl Shop in New Haven; Paul Macdonald, Sr., of David P. Ehrlich in Boston, and Paul Macdonald, Jr., of Leavitt & Peirce in Cambridge; Edmond Schulze and Randy Berger of the Smoke Shop in Southbury, Connecticut; Jordan Jarrar of Arcade Cigars in Fairfield, Connecticut; Michael Shulman at Archive Photos; and Rose Keyser at Time Inc. As always, thanks to J. Barry O'Rourke for the photographs, Laura Campbell for the elegant graphic design and Gerard Huerta for the exquisite hand-lettered title and cover art. Finally, our gratitude to Joel Fishman of Bedford Book Works, Inc., and to Joseph Montebello, Beth Bortz, Jennifer Ward and Mauro DiPreta at HarperCollins.

Contents

Introduction

Cigar lovers have always been collectors as much as smokers, keeping one eye on the cigar burning in the ashtray and the other eye on the rising and falling fortunes of their humidors. They know that cigars, like wine, improve with age. And, as with anything of value, they understand that collecting cigars is inextricably bound up with history and tradition, mystery and romance, memory and ceremony.

Since the mid-nineteenth century, connoisseurs have been laying down the best cigars to improve their smokability and as a hedge against shortages. At the onset of World War II, Winston Churchill arranged for the Romeo y Julietas and La Aroma de Cubas that he smoked to be shipped regularly from Havana to London. Eventually, he filled the walk-in humidor next to his office with more than 4,000 Cuban cigars. Equally with a mind on world events and collecting, shortly before signing the Cuban Trade Embargo, President John F. Kennedy dispatched Pierre Salinger to every smoke shop in Washington, D.C., to buy up 1,200 of the Upmann Petit Havanas he favored.

At the end of the twentieth century, cigar lovers are still doing everything they can to acquire the best cigars—a quest more challenging today perhaps than in the past. The Cuban embargo, limited production in some countries and a worldwide boom in demand have created unprecedented backorders for all premium cigars. At the same time, more manufacturers are introducing super-premium vintage and limited reserve editions, along with hundreds of new cigars a year. But the quest for the very best handmade cigars continues.

The twenty-two cigars shown on the following pages are among the best and most sought-after cigars in the world. Fewer than half of these are Cuban. The majority, which increasingly rival Cuban cigars in quality and flavor and outperform them in consistency, are from the Dominican Republic, Nicaragua, Honduras, even the United States. Several are cigars only a handful of men and women have ever smoked.

That isn't to say that these are the only cigars worth collecting or worthy of inclusion in a book on collecting cigars. Taste is subjective; one man's great smoke is another man's stogie. What's more, since tobacco is a natural product, made by human hands, any brand and size of cigar will vary in quality from season to season and frequently from box to box. The cigars listed and shown in the following pages are simply those named again and again by tobacco growers and blenders, rollers, retail store owners and collectors as being the best cigars in the world.

Naturally, your humidor will contain the cigars you enjoy smoking. These might be anything from pre-embargo Montecristo No. 1s bought for small fortunes at auction in London to inexpensive Arturo Fuente "Curlyheads" made last month in the Dominican Republic by third-level apprentice rollers with imperfect Chateau de la Fuente wrappers and blended Opus X and madura filler. But the complete humidor will also contain some, if not all, of the cigars found here.

This book is a concise guide to finding, acquiring and preserving great cigars. Of course, eventually even the rarest cigars must be smoked. And so this book is also a journal—an elegant, practical way of recording and comparing the cigars you've smoked: their origin, price, strength, flavor, burn, draw and ash. Moreover, it is a permanent place to affix the cigar bands for a visual record of your experiences and a personal album of glorious cigar art and history.

When exactly the right occasion arises, you'll go deep into your humidor and withdraw a Hoyo de Monterey Double Corona . . . or a Partagas Limited Reserve Robusto from the Dominican Republic . . . or a La Gloria Cubana Wavell made by expatriate Cuban rollers in Miami . . . or a Davidoff Dom Perignon from the El Laguito factory outside Havana when that cigar was still made there. And when these cigars have been reduced to ashes, you'll be able to recollect them, and the occasions on which they were smoked, and this period of your life, forever in the journal pages.

Collectors & Collecting

Collecting cigars is a temporal hobby and pleasure. Sooner or later—fifteen to twenty years at the latest—a cigar should be smoked. Although there is considerable debate over the quality and smokability of old Cuban cigars, after twenty years most cigars stop aging and begin to lose aroma, flavor and strength.

Until a few years ago, serious collectors were primarily interested in pre-confiscation or pre-embargo Havanas—those made in Cuba before Fidel Castro seized the country's major cigar companies in September of 1961 or before the United States imposed the trade embargo in January of 1962. Industry insiders and a handful of connoisseurs knew the value of these cigars and collected them accordingly. Edgar Cullman, Sr., chairman of Culbro Corp., which manufactures Macanudos and Partagas, has one of the largest collections of Cuban and pre-embargo cigars in the world, as does Marvin Shanken, the publisher of *Cigar Aficionado* magazine. Shelly Jacobs, a Minneapolis restaurateur, has collected several thousand boxes of Cuban and several hundred boxes of pre-embargo cigars over the past thirty years. Richard DiMeola, CEO of Consolidated Cigars, once owned nearly three thousand Belindas and Por Larrañagas from before 1958, but he smoked them.

But shortages of most premium cigars have made collectors out of most cigar lovers, and made most of the large-sized cigars now coming out of Cuba highly desirable and collectible. At the same time, the shortages and current boom have increased collectors' demand for vintage, limited reserve and limited production cigars from the Dominican Republic, Honduras, Nicaragua and the United States. In fact, almost any cigar of quality and size is now considered valuable and worth collecting. "Until a couple of years ago, I would've said you won't lose money collecting cigars, but you probably won't make a fortune," says Edward Sahakian of Davidoff in London. "Now I say, you won't lose money and you might make a little fortune."

Most pre-embargo Havanas have tripled in value since 1990, and recent Cuban cigars such as Trinidads and Cuban Davidoffs, both of which ceased production in the early '90s, have increased in value five and six times. Non-Cuban cigars, such as the one-time Partagas 150 Series, are also seen to be steadily accruing value.

More than financial investment, though, there is an almost mystical value to owning classic, handrolled cigars, antique humidors and cigar accoutrement. Marvin Shanken has said he got "caught up in the historical significance of the box" when he purchased John F. Kennedy's humidor at auction for $574,500. Similarly, a less-expensive humidor stocked with great cigars can also link young smokers with the master rollers, legendary brands and manufacturers and famous smokers of earlier eras.

When beginning a cigar collection, a general rule of thumb is that the larger the cigar and the darker the wrapper, the better it will age. All premium cigars these days, but particularly Cuban cigars, improve after even six months in a humidor. Buy regularly from one or two retail stores and develop a relationship with the manager or owner, so that he will put aside cigars for you. With the market for all handmade cigars tightening in the late 1990s, experts also advise laying down available cigars you enjoy now, and buying enough of them to age for five to seven years, when they will peak in flavor and strength.

In the end, good cigars possess one quality few other collectibles have. "It's not like a painting, where you either have to stare at it or sell it," notes Edward Sahakian. "The beauty of cigars is, if worse comes to worse, you can always smoke them."

Vintage, Limited Reserve & Limited Production Cigars

The collector's boom market of the 1990s has turned many handmade cigars into stars. It has also created several series of notable vintage cigars and produced some remarkable limited reserves.

Vintage and limited reserve cigars come from exceptional harvests and well-aged leaves, a process that produces considerably fewer units but cigars that are far richer, smoother and more complex than those turned out from three-month-old tobacco (the customary length of aging in the current market). One of the most popular vintage cigars released in the 1990s was General Cigar's **Partagas 150 Signature Series,** named in honor of the Partagas brand's 150th anniversary (the Partagas factory in Havana also produced a small number of special Partagas commemorating the anniversary in 1995.) The 150 Series cigars are made from Dominican filler but feature an eighteen-year-old Cameroon wrapper that was more a product of serendipity than planning. Alfonse Mayer, chief tobacco buyer for General Cigar, was in Madrid in September of 1994 when he met a leaf buyer for Tabacalera, Spain's tobacco monopoly, who mentioned he had a thousand bales of the aged Cameroon wrapper sitting in a warehouse. Mayer, who remembered the tobacco from an auction nearly two decades earlier, jumped at the chance to buy it.

The most prized of the 150 Series is the **Don Ramón,** a Churchill-sized cigar named after Ramón Cifuentes, whose family ran the Partagas factory in Havana before Castro took over and who oversaw production of Partagas in the Dominican Republic for many years. Only 10,000 Don

Partagas 150 Series Don Ramón & Partagas Limited Reserve Robusto

Ramóns were produced, the most limited quantity in the series. A one-time, total production of slightly under one million Partagas 150 cigars reportedly sold out the same day it went on sale in November of 1995, with collectors and market speculators sweeping up the bulk of the cigars. However, some retailers believe that a number of these cigars will reappear on the market at higher prices by the turn of the century.

Harder to find are **Partagas Limited Reserve** cigars. These are made from one-year-old Dominican leaves that pass through twenty-six processing stations after selection by Benjamin Menendez, a fourth-generation cigar man whose family once owned the H. Upmann factory in Havana. Only about 50,000 Partagas Limited Reserves are produced each year. The cigars are prized for their perfect, Cuban-like construction, and extraordinary richness and flavor. They come in humidor-quality boxes of twenty, with removable top trays, that are also collector's items. If, as *Cigar Aficionado*

has claimed, "it is difficult to notice the difference between a Dominican Partagas and a Cuban one," then Partagas Limited Reserves may make the distinction impossible.

Over the years, General Cigar has also introduced vintage selections of Macanudos—expertly constructed premium and super-premium cigars made with Mexican binder, Dominican and Mexican filler and Connecticut Shade wrapper—from the '79, '88 and '93 harvests. In December of 1995, the company reintroduced **Macanudo Vintage 1979,** a stronger, more complex smoke than non-vintage Macanudos. These are valuable cigars, with fewer than 35,000 produced from the last remaining bales of that year's harvest.

The most sought-after vintage series, however, and the one that experts claim comes closest to Cuban cigars in quality and strength, is the **Fuente-Fuente Opus X Series,** which was introduced late in 1995 and distributed only on the East Coast of the United States.

Every component of these cigars, including the Cuban-seed wrappers and filler that's aged from five to nine years, is grown on the one-hundred-and-fifty-acre Chateau de la Fuente and a few other farms in and around Santiago in the Dominican Republic. The distinctive reddish-brown Colorado wrappers and ornate bands distinguish these hard-to-find cigars. Only 75,000 cigars in seven sizes came on the market the first year, and 500,000 cigars in 1996, with 600,000 cigars and two additional sizes possible by late 1997, including an "A" measuring 9¼ inches long with a ring gauge of 52. In a blind tasting of figurados in 1996, *Cigar Aficionado* rated the Fuente-Fuente Opus X No. 2 second only to the Cuban Montecristo No. 2.

The success of the Fuente-Fuente Opus X Series has shown that superb, single-component cigars can be grown in the Dominican Republic, and that cigars from this and other countries now rival, and in some cases surpass, the best cigars coming out of Cuba.

A word about rating and acquiring cigars according to country of origin. In general, some countries produce stronger tobacco than others; wrapper leaves from Nicaragua or Cameroon, for example, tend to be darker and stronger than leaves grown in Connecticut or the Canary Islands. But that's about as far as generalization goes.

Wrappers, fillers and binders from specific countries "give some indication of the taste you can expect," says Hendrik Kelner, who produces premium and super-premium cigars in the Dominican Republic

Fuente Hemingway Masterpiece

for Davidoff, Avo, the Griffin and Paul Gamarian. "But different countries have different tastes, and each country has different regions with different tastes." A cigar's taste and strength are influenced by the soil, the climate and weather (the drier the season, the stronger the tobacco), the position of the leaf in the plant (bottom leaves have three times less nicotine than the top leaves), the tobacco grower, the curing process and the fermentation process. "Taste," Kelner adds, "is a combination of all these things."

Fuente also produces exceptional cigars in its Hemingway series, using tobacco aged a minimum of six months. Under Arturo Fuente, the company brought out the first Hemingways in the 1930s but stopped production by the mid-'70s, when the cigar industry slumped. Arturo then passed down his molds to his son, Don Carlos Fuente, the current chairman of the company, who taught his master rollers to make Hemingways in the early 1980s. Fewer than 5,000 **Fuente Hemingway Masterpieces,** measuring 8⅞ inches long with a ring gauge of 52, are made in any year.

Given the seemingly insatiable demand for super-premium cigars, a number of good to very good, low-production cigars are sought after by virtue of their quality and scarcity. Consolidated Cigar annually manufactures about a million Dominican-made Montecristos, for which Consolidated owns the trademark in the United States. Lighter in color and taste than Cuban

Fuente Fuente Opus X Fuente Fuente (left) & Reserva D'Chateau

Montecristos, the Consolidated version uses an aged Connecticut shade wrapper and selected Dominican binder and filler. Consolidated also produces the **Chairman Reserve,** a mild H. Upmann Lonsdale made specially for company chairman Ronald Perlman, that is 7 inches long with a ring gauge of 38 and comes individually packaged in a wood coffin. Introduced in 1996 at a retail price of $20, about 500,000 Chairman Reserves are planned for 1997.

Davidoff of Geneva also produces about a million **Davidoff Double "R"** cigars a year made from Dominican Republic binder and filler selected from different tobacco fields for a variety of flavors. The cigars, which are aged for up to four years and measure 7½ inches long with a ring gauge of 50, are exceptionally light, well-balanced smokes with a beautiful Connecticut shade wrapper and a wealth of taste.

Meanwhile, skilled expatriate Cuban rollers are turning out limited productions of good to great cigars in small factories in the United States. The best of these companies is Ernesto Perez-Carrillo's El Credito, based in Miami, which produces a version of an old Cuban cigar under its La Gloria Cubana brand. Following a feature story on the company in *Cigar Aficionado* in 1993, Perez-Carrillo saw sales skyrocket from about 600,000 cigars in 1990 to backorders of close to four million cigars in 1996, with customers flying in from all over the world to buy directly from his tiny storefront shop.

Davidoff Double "R" & Consolidated Cigar's Montecristo Robusto

La Gloria Cubana Wavell & Padrón Aniversario Exclusivo

The magazine rated the **La Gloria Cubana Wavell** one of the best robustos in the world. It and the other sizes in the line use blends of Sumatra-seed wrapper from Ecuador and binder and filler from Nicaragua, Brazil, Mexico and the Dominican Republic, where Perez-Carrillo opened a second factory in 1996.

Also in 1996, Cuba Aliados Cigars introduced a line of Puros Indios cigars made in Honduras under the direction of Don Rolando Reyes, Sr., a legendary cigar maker in Cuba, whose factory of the same name was seized by Castro's forces in 1968.

Rolled from aged, super-premium tobacco—Cuban-seed Ecuadoran wrappers and binder, and filler from the Dominican Republic, Nicaragua, Jamaica and Brazil—*Cigar Aficionado* gave the **Puros Indios Piramide No. 1** a 92 rating, one of the highest of any non-Cuban cigars. About half a million Puros Indios are made a year.

One small brand worth mentioning is Padrón Cigars. Based in Tampa, Padrón for most of its thirty years has made excellent cigars for the Cuban community in Florida. In 1994, the company released about 70,000 cigars in its **Padrón Aniversario Series** for national distribution. These are spicy, medium-strength, box-pressed cigars made from Cuban-seed Nicaraguan wrapper, binder and filler and aged three to four years. Less than 100,000 Padrón Aniversarios are produced annually.

❖

Cuban Cigars

One hundred years ago, more than a thousand cigar factories were operating in Cuba and many of the most famous brands were already in existence. Today, a half dozen factories produce a dozen or so of the major brands and the majority of premium and super-premium cigars coming out of the country. Scarcity of raw materials, poor harvests and rushed production in the 1990s have severely limited the output as well as the quality of Cuban cigars, and given them a reputation for inconsistency. Many smokers feel that Cuban cigars aren't what they used to be. At the same time, Dominican tobacco has been steadily improving in the forty-five years since Fidel Castro nationalized the factories and many of the old Cuban cigar families fled to the Dominican Republic, taking with them their knowledge, skills and tobacco seed.

Yet Cuban cigars are still made from Cuban tobacco, and Cuban wrapper leaves, in particular, still make for the richest and most flavorful smokes in the world. The belief holds that one cannot go to the grave without smoking a classic Cuban cigar. So highly regarded is Cuban tobacco and the abilities of Cuban rollers that even professionals associated with non-Cuban brands continue to sing their praises.

"The Dominican crop has improved and grown more consistent over the years," says General Cigar's Alfonse Mayer, one of the world's authorities on tobacco, "but it will never be the same as Cuban tobacco, and it will never be close enough. There's only one place where you can grow real

Hoyo de Monterrey Double Corona & Partagas Lusitania

Cuban tobacco for the real high, high quality cigars. Cuban tobacco is strong but still mellow, and the tender, loving care that goes into the manufacture of the cigars gives them a quality no one else can duplicate."

Besides, not since World War II have Cuban cigars been as sought-after by collectors, who will go almost anywhere, and pay almost anything, to acquire them. "The guys who can afford it know that there's no stock out there, and that there's not going to be, and they're buying up massive quantities of Cuban cigars," says Tom Hinds of Thomas Hinds Tobacconist in Toronto. Most of the better-known Cuban brands are in great demand: H. Upmann, Ramón Allones, Quai d'Orsay, El Rey del Mundo, Sancho Panza. But half a dozen or so Cuban cigars—benchmarks of their sizes—are prized above all others for their superior quality.

When it can be found, the Cuban cigar most favored by many collectors is the **Hoyo de Monterrey Double Corona.** Although it is the lightest of the

Cuban double coronas, this cigar's beautiful construction, fine bouquet and exquisite taste make it the most valued of the current Cuban cigars and worth laying down for long periods of time. The brand was founded by Jose Gener in the Vuelta Abajo region in 1865, and for many decades Hoyo de Monterreys have been made by the expert rollers at the La Corona factory in Havana. The double corona is the company's flagship cigar. In a blind tasting of double coronas in 1993, *Cigar Aficionado* awarded this Hoyo de Monterrey a 99.

Cohiba, despite complaints of inconsistency and massive quantities of inferior counterfeits, remains prized for its strength, its rich taste and, most of all, its legendary image. The choicest selection of harvests, three years of aging and a triple fermentation process endow the leaves used in these cigars with extraordinary smoothness and flavor. Fidel Castro is said to have smoked a lancero-sized Cohiba blended by Eduardo Ribera as early as 1959, but it wasn't until 1968 that three sizes of the blend were

Cohiba Robusto

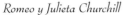
Romeo y Julieta Churchill

officially branded with the indigenous Cuban Indian word for cigar. Later, Avelino Lara developed and oversaw their production at El Laguito, the factory outside of Havana, where Cohibas were made by the highest-grade rollers exclusively for Castro as gifts for visiting foreign dignitaries. In the early '80s, Cubatabaco, the marketing department for Cuban cigars, responded to international demand and commercialized the brand. Today, nearly a dozen sizes are made at El Laguito and at several other factories in Havana. Once considered the pride of Cuba, Cohiba's quality problems in recent years have somewhat eroded its image, but the Cohiba Robusto and the Esplendido, a Churchill, remain fairly consistent and in great demand. A Dominican Cohiba (actually a Temple Hall with a different band) made by General Cigar is extremely mild by comparison.

The standard against which all Churchills continue to be measured is the **Romeo y Julieta,** the company that named the size for Sir Winston Churchill after World War

II. Other Churchills, such as the H. Upmann Sir Winston or the Cohiba Esplendido, are stronger smokes but Romeo y Julietas can have an extraordinary, complex finish and they are the most popular Churchills in Cuba. The company produces a variety of Churchills. Several of these are rounded and come packed in aluminum tubes, which keep them moist for a short time but don't allow them to age, and some of the rounded Romeo y Julietas are machine made but lack the words "De Luxe" on the tubes. Two of the Churchills that are box-pressed are known by different names and have slightly different blends: the Prince of Wales is the lightest of all Churchills; Clemenseaus, made in small quantities, are rich, robust Churchills with somewhat of a bitter aftertaste. Although Churchills made in other countries can vary in size, in Cuba they are made only in the size Sir Winston favored: 7 inches long with a ring gauge of 47.

Montecristos are the most popular and most produced of all Cuban brands. Along with Cohibas, they're also the most widely counterfeited; more fake No. 1s and No. 2s are believed to be on the market than real Montecristos. But the real items, both recent and pre-embargo, are among the best cigars made, due in part to their oily, Colorado claro wrappers, which age well and provide considerable taste and strength. Particularly prized by collectors is the **Montecristo No. 2,** a piramide, which measures 6⅛ inches long with a 52 ring gauge. Once rolled in Cuba (and after the confiscation, in the Canary Islands) by the legendary "Masinguila" (Jose Manuel Gonzalez), the No. 2 is one of the most difficult cigars to make and is now produced only by No. 6 rollers, the most sophisticated and qualified of rollers. The Montecristo No. 1, a lonsdale, is also very popular. Heavy demand and production may have diminished these cigars in recent years, but they are still distinctive, medium- to full-bodied smokes. Dominican Montecristos, made by Consolidated Cigar with a Connecticut shade wrapper, are milder but they are also being counterfeited in increasing numbers.

Partagas Lusitania is a connoisseur's double corona with a fuller, gutsier flavor than Hoyo de Monterreys of the same size, and the big gun in the line of more than forty handmade and machine-made Cuban Partagas. The brand, Cuba's second largest, has been produced in the same factory in downtown Havana since 1845. Dominican Partagas, and particularly the Partagas Special Reserves made by Benjamin Menendez for General Cigar, are equally excellent cigars with greater consistency and often superior construction.

Punch Punch & Montecristo No. 2

Punch Punch, a corona gorda measuring 5⅝ inches long with a ring gauge of 46, is the most famous of the Punch brand, which dates to 1840, and the benchmark of cigars of this size. Closer to a Churchill than a robusto, Punch Punch is a medium and spicy cigar, and if it isn't as rich as it once was, that's probably because few Cuban cigars are. A dozen and a half sizes of the brand are made at La Corona factory in Havana, with the Punch Churchill also highly valued as a smooth, flavorful smoke. Honduran-made Punch cigars are expertly constructed and flavorful.

Not as well known as other Cuban brands, **Bolivar** is a powerful, earthy and spicy cigar, made from the richest of all Cuban tobaccos and increasingly in demand by collectors. Named in honor of South American liberator Simón Bolívar, it is appreciated and collected for its powerful, full-bodied flavor and strong aroma. Yet Bolivars are also extremely well-balanced cigars, consistently smooth and easy to smoke. The cigars' dark, beautiful wrappers and big sizes—the 7 inch by 47 ring gauge Corona Gigantes, a Churchill; the torpedo-shaped 5½ inch by 52 ring gauge Belicoscos Finos; and the Royal Corona, a robusto—lend themselves to being laid down to age. "If I meet a man who says he smokes Bolivar Royal Coronas, there's nothing more I can do for him," says Hunters & Frankau's Simon Chase. "He's come to the edge of the firmament of cigars."

A complete listing of Cuban (and non-Cuban) cigars can be found in Anwer Bati and Simon Chase's excellent *The Cigar Companion: A Connoisseur's Guide.* Numerous articles on Cuba and Cuban cigars, along with blind tastings and ratings of those cigars, have appeared in Marvin Shanken's *Cigar Aficionado* and the sister newsletter, *Cigar Insider.* Shanken also publishes a separate *Buying Guide to Cuban Cigars.*

Bolivar Corona Gigantes

Pre-Embargo Havanas

Montecristo No. 1 from the late 1950s

The value of pre-embargo cigars lies in their great rarity (expatriate Cuban cigar makers may prefer the term "pre-confiscation," but pre-embargo is generally used to describe Cuban cigars made before 1962). Only a very few have survived to the present day. The very rarest of these cigars are from brands that no longer exist, and most were made by master rollers who are no longer alive.

Desmond Sautter, who has specialized in old Cuban cigars for a number of years, once had some 10,000 pre-embargos in his London shop. The great demand for old Cuban cigars in the 1990s has reduced that number to fewer than 100 boxes and has also limited the number of calls Sautter receives from people looking to sell old boxes that they've found or inherited. Most people, he says, prefer to auction them for increasingly higher prices. The average cost for a box of twenty-five at Sautter's is about $1,500. The bigger the cigar and the more unusual the brand, size or shape, the more expensive they tend to be.

Since 1990, demand for pre-embargos has caused prices to rise by as much as 1,000 percent. Before the current boom, old Cuban cigars typically were less expensive than post-embargo cigars. Sometimes they were given away, with collectors interested solely in the boxes and label art. Compare that to the several 1996 auctions in London where Montecristo No. 2s sold for the equivalent of $161 apiece, and Romeo y Julieta Gigantes Extras for $109 each.

While everyone in the industry has witnessed the recent frenzy for pre-embargos, experts disagree on the subject of their smokability. The youngest of these cigars are now forty-five years old, well past their prime. As might be expected, many smokers find them overly dry, musty and, as with more recent Cuban cigars, frequently buggy or moldy. Detractors believe that history and mystique have created the craze for old cigars, not their taste.

Yet those who collect old Cuban cigars,

especially the best brands and biggest sizes, believe they possess flavor and craftsmanship rarely matched by post-embargo cigars. They point to the fact that a Montecristo No. 1 from 1958, like the one shown in the photograph on the previous page, scored a 98 in a blind tasting conducted by *Cigar Aficionado* in late 1993—a considerably higher rating than that awarded other, more recent Montecristos. "Old cigars don't go down in smokability, they change," notes Shelly Jacobs, whose collection of pre-embargos includes a box from 1890. "They're complex, and some are delicious."

Where does one find old Cuban cigars these days? Authorities advise collectors to follow auctions in major European cities, especially London, where Christie's and Sotheby's periodically auction pre-embargos. Christie's publishes a monthly catalog of its cigar auctions, as does *Cigar Insider,* along with the cigars to be offered and pre-sale estimates. In the United States, charity dinners occasionally feature pre-embargo cigars, and collectors, though far less frequently, offer them for sale through a cigar retailer or cigar publication.

When pre-embargos can be found, however, there is no guarantee that they've been kept in optimum conditions over the past four or more decades; if they've been too dry for too long and have lost their essential oils, they will be beyond reviving and will prove to be extremely dry smokes. Some established retail stores in Great Britain, France, Switzerland and Spain still have limited inventories of pre-embargos, which tend to be in better condition than those bought at auction.

American citizens can legally bring pre-embargo cigars into the United States, since they pre-date the 1962 trade embargo. But experts caution against expecting an easy time. Desmond Sautter once sold a box of rare pre-embargos to an American customer, taking care to supply a certificate establishing their age. United States Customs officials confiscated the cigars, claiming that the certificate proved the legality of the box but not necessarily the contents.

Other Prized Cigars

Stacked on cedar shelves in the second-floor, walk-in humidor at Nat Sherman's Fifth Avenue store in New York City are box after box of customers' cigars that are no longer on the market. Some of these are recent, limited production cigars, such as the 30,000 Partagas 150 Series one customer laid down for himself and his son; others, like the single box of Casa Buenas from the Canary Islands, haven't been made in many years. The unavailability of these and other cigars makes them all the more desirable, causing collectors to call Nat Sherman's regularly to inquire about the health of longtime customers who keep their cigars in the store's humidor.

In 1991, Davidoff of Geneva stopped producing cigars in Cuba because of what the company says were quality issues. Cuban Davidoffs instantly became sought after by smokers around the world, and **Davidoff Dom Perignons** tripled in price. That has only inspired cigar lovers to buy up whatever quantities they can find of these elegant, Churchill-sized cigars, which many consider the best ever made. The company is sitting on a large supply of the real thing in Geneva, but according to the terms of an agreement it signed with Cuba, none can be sold. Collectors, meanwhile, occasionally find them in out-of-the-way shops in Europe. "You might come across one or two in a small tobacconist's in a village in England that have been there for twenty years," says Edward Sahakian, "but this is getting rarer and rarer." The majority of Cuban Davidoffs turning up in auctions are believed to be counterfeit.

Davidoff Dom Perignons

Trinidad

A more fabled smoke, and perhaps the most-prized cigar in the world, is the **Trinidad,** a single-sized cigar produced in Cuba in extremely limited quantities for the King of Spain and other foreign dignitaries. Named for a historic city on the island's west coast, the Trinidad is essentially an earthier Cohiba Lancero—7½ inches long with a 38 ring gauge—using a darker, higher-quality wrapper, a blend of tobaccos similar to Partagas and a new band. What is believed to be a fourth fermentation gives Trinidads extraordinary smoothness, along with a reputation among Cubans for being superior to Cohibas. Fidel Castro has claimed no knowledge of the cigar, and workers at the El Laguito factory, where Trinidads are produced, say someone else in the government began ordering the cigars in cedar boxes of 100 as special gifts after Cohibas were commercialized. An article that appeared in the first issue of *Cigar Aficionado,* entitled "Trinidad: The Best Kept Secret in Cuba," created so much publicity and demand for the cigars that production was believed to have been stopped in 1993. But several hundred Trinidads were served at a charitable dinner in Paris in the fall of 1995, and boxes of 50 are still being given to foreign dignitaries. They also showed up on the black market in 1996 for $4,000 for a box of 25.

Another cigar few people are likely to see, much less store in their humidors or smoke at home, is a special H. Upmann created in 1995 for President Bill Clinton. Although Consolidated Cigar has publicly disclaimed its existence, the company began sending the White House boxes of **Presidential Upmanns,** bearing the presidential seal, after Air Force Captain Scott O'Grady was rescued from Bosnia and the president reportedly told aides he was going out on the back porch to celebrate by smoking a cigar.

Master tobacco blenders continually roll cigars for themselves to sample harvests and try new blends or for their own enjoyment. Cigar lovers lucky enough to meet and befriend these professionals may find themselves the recipients of their private reserves. They are perhaps the most desirable collectibles of all, since they represent tradition, passion and quality in the purest form.

Carlos Fuente, Sr., chairman of A. Fuente y Cia, learned how to roll cigars from his father, Arturo, and inherited his cigar molds. In the early 1980s, Don Carlos revived a blend and line of cigars Arturo Fuente had helped originate, the Hemingway series of cigars, by passing on his knowledge and skills to master rollers like Luis Rosario. The patriarch of the Fuente family occasionally still rolls superbly constructed, classic Cuban cigars, like the pyramid shown on this page, from tobacco grown at Chateau de la Fuente in the Dominican Republic.

Benjamin Menendez, who as a young man watched the great Masinguila roll cigars in the factory the Menendez family owned in Havana, makes about fifty cigars a year for himself entirely from Dominican tobacco. These single-component coronas, which predate the Fuentes' success in producing superior, all-Domincan cigars, appear casually made, as if Benji—as he is known throughout the industry—had walked through the curing barns selecting, bunching and rolling leaves as he went. Yet his cigars are remarkable smokes, with a light start with fruit flavors and a remarkably rich and complex finish, and as good as any Cuban corona.

❖

Don Carlos Fuente Personal Reserve (left) & Benji Menendez Personal Reserve

Counterfeits

Counterfeit Cuban and non-Cuban cigars have been flooding the market in growing numbers in recent years. The worldwide shortage of big cigars, the continuing illegality of Cuban cigars in the United States and the huge profits to be made by counterfeiters contribute to the problem.

The most popular and widely counterfeited Cuban cigars are Cohibas and Montecristos, followed by Dominican versions of the same brands. Fake Cuban Davidoffs, especially Dom Perignons and Aniversarios, have also been appearing in large numbers in Europe. As the prices of all valuable cigars continue to soar, counterfeits are becoming increasingly more difficult to detect. Some counterfeiters have gotten hold of the original molds used to make Cuban Davidoff boxes. There is also rumor of a factory in Venezuela that turns out new counterfeit cigar boxes. Sophisticated counterfeiters are copying the factory code numbers on the bottoms of the boxes and using better inks to duplicate the bands.

Retailers recommend never buying cigars sold on the street or priced too cheap, or from anyone but a reputable source. They also suggest not buying the heavily counterfeited brands. Even then, how can buyers be sure what they're buying isn't fake? Experts say there are many ways to tell. The ink on counterfeit boxes is frequently smudged, something Cuban manufacturers never do. In inferior counterfeits, the color and ring gauges of the cigars in a single box vary. Fake Cuban boxes often come without a sticker on the inside lid, or without paper or promotional material. The crest on the label may not be folded exactly in the middle of the seal, a practice in Cuban factories, or no half moon is cut out of the corner of the cedar strip between the layers of cigars to make it easier to lift out.

There are also telltale signs with the cigars themselves. The wrappers on counterfeits can vary in color or are greenish or spotted. Construction is sometimes visibly poor, and when the box is opened the cigars give off a smell of ammonia, indicating that the tobacco is raw and unaged or unfermented. Although the tobacco is Cuban and the cigars are probably smokable, they're clearly not the blends advertised.

Preserving Great Cigars

The countries that grow the best tobacco in the world are natural humidors; a cigar left outside over night in Cuba or the Dominican Republic will be moist and perfectly smokable the next day, and the day after that. Elsewhere, however, cigars must be stored in an artificially warm and humid environment if they are to stay moist, age properly and remain at their peak smokability.

Humidors—boxes lined usually with cedar and outfitted with a humidification device—do just that. Some retailers believe that cigars should be smoked soon after being shipped from the factory, and they recommend that customers buy only what they can smoke within a month or two. But the idea of a humidor isn't to keep cigars factory-fresh so much as it is to prevent them from drying out and to help the filler, binder and wrapper continue to blend or marry.

When considering buying a humidor, look first for a solidly built box with square, smooth corner joints and a tight-fitting top that will keep humidity in and outside air out. Although some in the industry believe cedar imparts its odor to cigars, most feel it retains moisture more than other woods and enhances the aging process. Antique humidors are in demand and can occasionally be found in antique and consignment shops or at auction, but experts caution against their use. If they're antiques, they say, it's likely that they weren't built as humidors and won't close tightly. And if they are authentic, early humidors, they're probably lined with tin, which can rust, or copper, which can oxidize, tainting the taste of the cigars.

Also popular are Tupperware containers outfitted with small humidifiers. These can be practical as very inexpensive, short-term humidors but are unsuitable for presenting fine cigars or when discussing the subject of humidors with serious cigar smokers. "If you treasure your cigars, I wouldn't recommend them," says Graves "Smitty" Smith, who manages the humidor at Nat Sherman's Fifth Avenue store in New York City. "It's like storing a fine bottle of wine in your refrigerator. Cigars need humidity and they need cedar to absorb moisture and help them age. Don't mention Tupperware to me."

In the end, if you've gone to the trouble and expense of acquiring the best cigars in the world, it pays to invest in the best humidor you can afford.

The ideal climate inside a humidor is a constant 65 to 70 degrees and 70 percent humidity. Pre-embargo cigars do better in cooler and slightly drier conditions: 60 to 65 degrees and 65 to 67 percent humidity. (If cigars have dried to the point of losing their essential oils, however, no amount of humidity will bring them back.) In addition to humidification devices, some humidors come with hygrometers, which gauge humidity, but they are generally unreliable. "They don't really mean anything," says Smitty. "You have to feel the cigars, and listen to them, and smell them. The aroma will tell you if a cigar is flat and dry or not."

A humidor that maintains the proper temperature and humidity will keep cigars moist enough to retain their oils and dry enough to retard mold. Lew Rothman of JR Tobacco also suggests periodically wiping the inside of the humidor with white vinegar diluted with water, then setting it out for a while in the sun, in order to prevent mold.

Once cigars are laid down in a humidor, no one knows for sure what happens to them. While most professionals believe that tobaccos continue to marry in a humidor, with the oils from the wrapper leaves permeating the binder and filler, some feel that different cigars stored together in the same humidor will inter-marry, so that after six months or so they'll all taste the same. The reality is probably that lighter, weaker cigars will eventually pick up some taste and flavor from stronger cigars but strong cigars will still taste strong after six months or longer.

However, cigars do marry and age better when laid down in numbers, and experts recommend humidifying quantities of twenty-five or fifty of the same cigars in separate humidors or in their own boxes on cedar shelves. Most cigar smokers, of course, can't afford numerous humidors or walk-in humidors. Fortunately, established retail cigar shops will humidify cigars bought through the store, indefinitely and free of charge, for regular customers.

The Handmade Cigar Collector's

Journal

Affix label here

Brand:

Country:

Length:

Strength:

Burn:

Flavor:

Description:

Ring Gauge:

Draw:

Ash:

Personal Rating (1–10):

Venue:

Price:

Thoughts and Reminiscences:

Winston Churchill

From the age of 20, when he was a junior army officer stationed in Havana, until his death at 92, Winston Churchill smoked the very best cigars—mainly Romeo y Julietas and La Aroma de Cubas—and as many as ten of them a day. Sir Winston's personal humidor of some 4,000 cigars led his valet to remark that the British Prime Minister's "weekly cigar allowance is equal to my annual salary." Churchill led Britain through the dark days of World War II and was awarded the Nobel Prize in Literature. The Romeo y Julieta factory in Havana named its No. 10 cigar in his honor.

Brand:

Country:

Length:

Strength:

Burn:

Flavor:

Description:

Ring Gauge:

Draw:

Ash:

Personal Rating (1–10):

Venue:

Price:

Thoughts and Reminiscences:

Affix label here

Brand: ....

Country: .... Description: ....

Length: .... Ring Gauge: ....

Strength: .... Draw: ....

Burn: .... Ash: ....

Flavor: ....

....

....

Personal Rating (1–10): ....

Venue: .... Price: ....

Thoughts and Reminiscences: ....

....

....

....

....

....

....

Affix label here

Affix label here

Brand:

Country:

Length:

Strength:

Burn:

Flavor:

Description:

Ring Gauge:

Draw:

Ash:

Personal Rating (1–10):

Venue:

Price:

Thoughts and Reminiscences:

Alfred Hitchcock

Alfred Hitchcock worked as a title designer in films for five years before getting a chance to direct his first feature. With his third film, The Lodger, *in 1926, he introduced his bold visual style and the recurrent theme of ordinary men caught in a web of extraordinary events. He went on to direct such classics as* The Man Who Knew Too Much, The Thirty-Nine Steps, North by Northwest *and* Rear Window. *Hitchcock was an avid smoker of Cuban Montecristos.*

Brand:

Country:

Length:

Strength:

Burn:

Flavor:

Description:

Ring Gauge:

Draw:

Ash:

Personal Rating (1–10):

Venue:

Price:

Thoughts and Reminiscences:

Affix label here

Affix label here

Brand: ....

Country: ....

Length: ....

Strength: ....

Burn: ....

Flavor: ....

....

....

Personal Rating (1–10): ....

Venue: ....

Thoughts and Reminiscences: ....

....

....

....

....

....

....

....

Description: ....

Ring Gauge: ....

Draw: ....

Ash: ....

....

....

Price: ....

Affix label here

Brand:

Country:

Length:

Strength:

Burn:

Flavor:

Personal Rating (1–10):

Venue:

Thoughts and Reminiscences:

Description:

Ring Gauge:

Draw:

Ash:

Price:

Ernie Kovacs

One of television's truly original comedians, Kovacs wrote most of the material for The Ernie Kovacs Show, *a live hit of the 1950s that showcased his offbeat, improvisational sense of humor. Appearing with actress/wife Edie Adams, Kovacs was rarely seen without a cigar, and even appeared as one of the Dutch Masters in ads for the cigar manufacturer of the same name who sponsored the show. He also appeared in ten movies before his death at 43.*

Brand:

Country:

Length:

Strength:

Burn:

Flavor:

Description:

Ring Gauge:

Draw:

Ash:

Personal Rating (1–10):

Venue:

Price:

Thoughts and Reminiscences:

Affix label here

Brand:

Country: Description:

Length: Ring Gauge:

Strength: Draw:

Burn: Ash:

Flavor:

Personal Rating (1–10):

Venue: Price:

Thoughts and Reminiscences:

Affix label here

Affix label here

Brand:

Country:

Length:

Strength:

Burn:

Flavor:

Description:

Ring Gauge:

Draw:

Ash:

Personal Rating (1–10):

Venue:

Price:

Thoughts and Reminiscences:

Samuel Clemens

Whether as himself or under his pen name, Mark Twain, the author of The Adventures of Huckleberry Finn *and other American classics, said he picked a cigar up off the sidewalk when he was nine and never stopped smoking. He smoked as many as thirty cigars a day, occasionally Havanas but more frequently American-made cigars. When chastised for his habit, he liked to point out, "I smoke in moderation. Only one cigar at a time."*

Brand:
....

Country:
....

Length:
....

Strength:
....

Burn:
....

Flavor:
....
....
....

Personal Rating (1–10):

Venue:
....

Thoughts and Reminiscences:
....
....
....
....
....
....
....

Description:
....

Ring Gauge:
....

Draw:
....

Ash:
....
....
....

Price:
....

Affix label here

Affix label here

Brand: ....

Country: ....

Length: ....

Strength: ....

Burn: ....

Flavor: ....

....

....

Description: ....

Ring Gauge: ....

Draw: ....

Ash: ....

....

....

Personal Rating (1–10): ....

Venue: ....

Price: ....

Thoughts and Reminiscences: ....

....

....

....

....

....

....

Affix label here

Brand:

Country:

Length:

Strength:

Burn:

Flavor:

Description:

Ring Gauge:

Draw:

Ash:

Personal Rating (1–10):

Venue:

Price:

Thoughts and Reminiscences:

Ulysses S. Grant

When General Ulysses S. Grant was elected the eighteenth president of the United States, he continued a long tradition of commanders-in-chief who smoked cigars. After newspapers reported him lighting up in the midst of one Civil War battle, Grant received gifts of some 10,000 boxes of cigars. In perhaps the most decisive battle of that war, Grant brought Robert E. Lee's Confederate Army to its knees and, ultimately, to surrender at Appomattox.

Brand:

Country:

Length:

Strength:

Burn:

Flavor:

Description:

Ring Gauge:

Draw:

Ash:

Personal Rating (1–10):

Venue:

Price:

Thoughts and Reminiscences:

Affix label here

Brand: ....

Country: .... Description: ....

Length: .... Ring Gauge: ....

Strength: .... Draw: ....

Burn: .... Ash: ....

Flavor: ....

....

....

....

Personal Rating (1–10): ....

Venue: .... Price: ....

Thoughts and Reminiscences: ....

....

....

....

....

....

....

Affix label here

Affix label here

Brand: ....

Country: ....

Length: ....

Strength: ....

Burn: ....

Flavor: ....

....

....

Description: ....

Ring Gauge: ....

Draw: ....

Ash: ....

....

....

....

Personal Rating (1–10): ....

Venue: ....

Price: ....

Thoughts and Reminiscences: ....

....

....

....

George Burns

Born Nathan Birnbaum in New York in 1896, George Burns worked for years in vaudeville before teaming up with the love of his life, Gracie Allen. Together, Burns and Allen starred on stage, radio, in film and television. In 1975, Burns won an Oscar for his role in Neil Simon's The Sunshine Boys. *Of his consumption of ten to fifteen El Productos a day he quipped, "If I'd taken my doctor's advice and quit smoking, I wouldn't have lived to go to his funeral." George Burns died in 1996 at the age of 100.*

Brand: ....

Country: ....

Description: ....

Length: ....

Ring Gauge: ....

Strength: ....

Draw: ....

Burn: ....

Ash: ....

Flavor: ....

....

....

....

....

Personal Rating (1–10): ....

Venue: ....

Price: ....

Thoughts and Reminiscences: ....

....

....

....

....

....

....

Affix label here

Affix label here

Brand:

Country:

Length:

Strength:

Burn:

Flavor:

Description:

Ring Gauge:

Draw:

Ash:

Personal Rating (1–10):

Venue:

Price:

Thoughts and Reminiscences:

Affix label here

Brand: ....

Country: ....

Length: ....

Strength: ....

Burn: ....

Flavor: ....
....
....

Personal Rating (1–10): ....

Venue: ....

Thoughts and Reminiscences: ....

Description: ....

Ring Gauge: ....

Draw: ....

Ash: ....
....
....
....

Price: ....

....
....
....

Ernest Hemingway

The most famous of the expatriate Americans living in Paris in the 1920s, Hemingway's novel The Sun Also Rises, *published when he was just 26, firmly established his reputation as the most influential writer of his times. For many years Hemingway lived in Cuba, where he had unlimited access to bullfights, rum and Cuban cigars, befitting his self-imposed macho image. He received the Nobel Prize in Literature in 1954.*

Brand: ....

Country: ....

Length: ....

Strength: ....

Burn: ....

Flavor: ....

Description: ....

Ring Gauge: ....

Draw: ....

Ash: ....

....

....

....

Personal Rating (1–10): ....

Venue: ....

Price: ....

Thoughts and Reminiscences: ....

....

....

....

....

....

....

....

Affix label here

Brand:

Country:

Length:

Strength:

Burn:

Flavor:

Description:

Ring Gauge:

Draw:

Ash:

Personal Rating (1–10):

Venue:

Price:

Thoughts and Reminiscences:

Affix label here

Affix label here

Brand: ....

Country: ....

Length: ....

Strength: ....

Burn: ....

Flavor: ....

....

....

Personal Rating (1–10): ....

Venue: ....

Thoughts and Reminiscences: ....

....

....

....

Description: ....

Ring Gauge: ....

Draw: ....

Ash: ....

....

....

....

Price: ....

Virginia Woolf

One of the bright lights of the celebrated Bloomsbury circle, English writer Virginia Woolf was sensitive to the point of frequent breakdowns but independent enough to smoke cigars at a time when few women did. Her most influential works, which appeared in the 1920s, include the novels To the Lighthouse *and* Orlando; *and* A Room of One's Own, *a feminist pamphlet. Under the strain of World War II, Woolf drowned herself in 1941.*

Brand: ....

Country: ....   Description: ....

Length: ....   Ring Gauge: ....

Strength: ....   Draw: ....

Burn: ....   Ash: ....

Flavor: ....

....

....

Personal Rating (1–10): ....

Venue: ....   Price: ....

Thoughts and Reminiscences: ....

....

....

....

....

....

....

Affix label here

Affix label here

Brand:

Country:

Length:

Strength:

Burn:

Flavor:

Description:

Ring Gauge:

Draw:

Ash:

Personal Rating (1–10):

Venue:

Price:

Thoughts and Reminiscences:

Affix label here

Brand:

Country:

Length:

Strength:

Burn:

Flavor:

Description:

Ring Gauge:

Draw:

Ash:

Personal Rating (1–10):

Venue:

Price:

Thoughts and Reminiscences:

Sigmund Freud

The father of psychoanalysis, Freud analyzed patients and wrote The Interpretation of Dreams *while smoking up to twenty cigars a day. He favored Don Pedros and Reina Cubanas but also Dutch Liliputanos. Freud tirelessly praised the ritual and pleasure of cigar smoking, as well as its place in his intellectual life. "I owe to the cigar," he wrote, "a great intensification of my capacity to work and a facilitation of my self-control."*

Brand:

Country: Description:

Length: Ring Gauge:

Strength: Draw:

Burn: Ash:

Flavor:

Personal Rating (1–10):

Venue: Price:

Thoughts and Reminiscences:

Affix label here

Brand:

Country: Description:

Length: Ring Gauge:

Strength: Draw:

Burn: Ash:

Flavor:

Personal Rating (1–10):

Venue: Price:

Thoughts and Reminiscences:

Affix label here

Affix label here

Brand:

Country:

Length:

Strength:

Burn:

Flavor:

Description:

Ring Gauge:

Draw:

Ash:

Personal Rating (1–10):

Venue:

Price:

Thoughts and Reminiscences:

Milton Berle

A cruise to Havana in 1920 as a young actor hooked Milton Berle on Cuban cigars. Since then, he has been as well-known for his cigar smoking as for his antic comedy routines. Berle starred in vaudeville, radio, nightclubs, films and became television's first superstar as master of ceremonies of the Texaco Star Theatre from the late 1940s to the late '50s. Uncle Miltie, who loved Upmann Amatistas, Romeo y Julietas and Cohibas, among other Havanas, gave John F. Kennedy the now-famous humidor bought at auction by Marvin Shanken in 1996.

Brand:
....

Country: ....

Length: ....

Strength: ....

Burn: ....

Flavor: ....

....

....

....

Description: ....

Ring Gauge: ....

Draw: ....

Ash: ....

....

....

Personal Rating (1–10): ....

Venue: ....

Price: ....

Thoughts and Reminiscences: ....

....

....

....

....

....

....

Affix label here

Affix label here

Brand: ....

Country: ....

Length: ....

Strength: ....

Burn: ....

Flavor: ....

....

Personal Rating (1–10): ....

Venue: ....

Thoughts and Reminiscences: ....

....

....

....

....

....

....

Description: ....

Ring Gauge: ....

Draw: ....

Ash: ....

....

....

....

Price: ....

Affix label here

Brand:

Country:

Length:

Strength:

Burn:

Flavor:

Description:

Ring Gauge:

Draw:

Ash:

Personal Rating (1–10):

Venue:

Thoughts and Reminiscences:

Price:

Evelyn Waugh

Waugh, the British-born author of Decline and Fall *and* The Loved One, *was educated at Oxford where he reportedly spent much of his undergraduate days drinking, socializing and smoking cigars. Later, he drew on real life characters and cigars for his most famous novel,* Brideshead Revisited, *in which he immortalized Havana Partagas. "The most futile and disastrous day seems well spent," Waugh wrote, "when it is reviewed through the blue, fragrant smoke of a Havana cigar."*

Brand:

Country:

Length:

Strength:

Burn:

Flavor:

Personal Rating (1–10):

Venue:

Thoughts and Reminiscences:

Description:

Ring Gauge:

Draw:

Ash:

Price:

Affix label here

Brand:
....

Country: Description:
....

Length: Ring Gauge:
....

Strength: Draw:
....

Burn: Ash:
....

Flavor:
....

....

....

Personal Rating (1–10):
....

Venue: Price:
....

Thoughts and Reminiscences:
....

....

....

....

....

Affix label here

Affix label here

Brand:

Country:

Length:

Strength:

Burn:

Flavor:

Personal Rating (1–10):

Venue:

Thoughts and Reminiscences:

Description:

Ring Gauge:

Draw:

Ash:

Price:

Colette

The early-twentieth-century author of Claudine in Paris *and other fiction based on her life, Sidonie Gabrielle Colette was as famous for her independence as for her writing. A sensualist as well as a feminist, she shocked French society by carrying on a highly publicized affair with a much younger man and smoking cigars in public. Her last novel,* Gigi, *published in 1944, was turned into an Academy Award– winning film. Upon her death in 1954, she was the first woman in France to be accorded a state funeral.*

Brand: ....

Country: ....   Description: ....

Length: ....   Ring Gauge: ....

Strength: ....   Draw: ....

Burn: ....   Ash: ....

Flavor: ....

....

....

Personal Rating (1–10): ....

Venue: ....   Price: ....

Thoughts and Reminiscences: ....

....

....

....

....

....

....

Affix label here

Affix label here

Brand: ....

Country: ....

Length: ....

Strength: ....

Burn: ....

Flavor: ....

....

Description: ....

Ring Gauge: ....

Draw: ....

Ash: ....

....

....

....

Personal Rating (1–10): ....

Venue: ....

Price: ....

Thoughts and Reminiscences:

....

....

....

....

....

....

....

Affix label here

Brand:

Country:

Length:

Strength:

Burn:

Flavor:

Description:

Ring Gauge:

Draw:

Ash:

Personal Rating (1–10):

Venue:

Price:

Thoughts and Reminiscences:

H. L. Mencken

Henry Louis Mencken worked in his father's cigar factory in Baltimore for just a year before quitting to write for the Baltimore Sun. Soon, he was the most-famous American editor and critic of the first half of the twentieth century and was, in the words of Alistair Cooke, "the most volcanic newspaperman this country has ever known." Mencken was also a fiery advocate of civil rights, freedom of speech and freedom to smoke. He enjoyed domestic five-cent cigars but also rolled his own from choice Havana leaves.

Brand:

Country:

Length:

Strength:

Burn:

Flavor:

Description:

Ring Gauge:

Draw:

Ash:

Personal Rating (1–10):

Venue:

Price:

Thoughts and Reminiscences:

Affix label here

Brand: ....

Country: .... Description: ....

Length: .... Ring Gauge: ....

Strength: .... Draw: ....

Burn: .... Ash: ....

Flavor: ....

....

....

Personal Rating (1–10): ....

Venue: .... Price: ....

Thoughts and Reminiscences: ....

....

....

....

....

....

Affix label here

Affix label here

Brand: ....

Country: ....

Length: ....

Strength: ....

Burn: ....

Flavor: ....

....

....

Description: ....

Ring Gauge: ....

Draw: ....

Ash: ....

....

....

Personal Rating (1–10): ....

Venue: ....

Price: ....

Thoughts and Reminiscences: ....

....

....

....

Henry Clay

U.S. Senator Henry Clay, known as "The Great Compromiser" and "The Great Pacificator," gained early prominence as defense counsel for Aaron Burr and later was named Speaker of the House, a position he held for many years. Despite his skills in compromise and settlement, in 1826 Clay fought a duel with John Randolph over unsubstantiated charges of corrupt bargaining. Henry Clay cigars, one of the most famous of the old Havana brands, were named after the senator, who had business interests in Cuba.

Brand:

Country:

Description:

Length:

Ring Gauge:

Strength:

Draw:

Burn:

Ash:

Flavor:

Personal Rating (1–10):

Venue:

Price:

Thoughts and Reminiscences:

Affix label here

Affix label here

Brand:

Country:

Length:

Strength:

Burn:

Flavor:

Personal Rating (1–10):

Venue:

Thoughts and Reminiscences:

Description:

Ring Gauge:

Draw:

Ash:

Price:

Affix label here

Brand:

Country:

Length:

Strength:

Burn:

Flavor:

Description:

Ring Gauge:

Draw:

Ash:

Personal Rating (1–10):

Venue:

Price:

Thoughts and Reminiscences:

John F. Kennedy

JFK developed a taste for cigars as an undergraduate at Harvard and favored H. Upmann Petit Havanas while in office. As the thirty-eighth president of the United States, Kennedy was immensely popular at home and abroad for his youth, vigor and wit, but his term in office was tested by the disastrous Bay of Pigs attempted invasion and the Cuban missile crisis of 1962. Although he signed the trade embargo banning cigars, among other Cuban products, from entering the United States, Kennedy remained a fan of Havanas.

Brand:

Country:

Length:

Strength:

Burn:

Flavor:

Personal Rating (1–10):

Venue:

Thoughts and Reminiscences:

Description:

Ring Gauge:

Draw:

Ash:

Price:

Affix label here

Brand: ....

Country: ....

Length: ....

Strength: ....

Burn: ....

Flavor: ....

....

....

Description: ....

Ring Gauge: ....

Draw: ....

Ash: ....

....

....

....

Personal Rating (1–10): ....

Venue: ....

Thoughts and Reminiscences: ....

....

....

....

....

....

....

Price: ....

Affix label here

Affix label here

Brand:

Country:

Length:

Strength:

Burn:

Flavor:

Description:

Ring Gauge:

Draw:

Ash:

Personal Rating (1–10):

Venue:

Price:

Thoughts and Reminiscences:

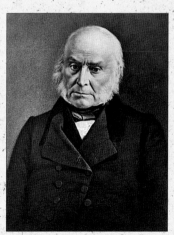

John Quincy Adams

The cigar-smoking son of a U.S. president, John Quincy Adams was a politician of fierce independence. Nicknamed "Old Man Eloquent" for his speaking skills, Adams proposed the first antislavery legislation, helped draft the Monroe Doctrine and pushed through a treaty with Spain in 1819 that ceded Florida to the U.S. He was elected the sixth president of the United States in 1824.

Brand:
....

Country: Description:
....

Length: Ring Gauge:
....

Strength: Draw:
....

Burn: Ash:
....

Flavor:
....

....

....

Personal Rating (1–10):
....

Venue: Price:
....

Thoughts and Reminiscences:
....

....

....

....

....

....

....

Affix label here

Affix label here

Brand:

Country: Description:

Length: Ring Gauge:

Strength: Draw:

Burn: Ash:

Flavor:

Personal Rating (1–10):

Venue: Price:

Thoughts and Reminiscences:

Affix label here

Brand:

Country: Description:

Length: Ring Gauge:

Strength: Draw:

Burn: Ash:

Flavor:

Personal Rating (1–10):

Venue: Price:

Thoughts and Reminiscences:

Fidel Castro

As a young lawyer practicing in Havana, Fidel Castro embraced liberal and democratic ideals but became a revolutionary after Fulgencio Batista staged a coup d'état in 1952. Later, Castro hid in the mountains with Che Guevara, plotting the overthrow of the Batista dictatorship and smoking the earliest Cohibas, which were made for him. A survivor of the attempted Bay of Pigs invasion and the United States trade embargo, Castro has said he favors a reconciliation with the U.S.

Brand: ....

Country: ....

Length: ....

Strength: ....

Burn: ....

Flavor: ....

....

....

Personal Rating (1–10): ....

Venue: ....

Thoughts and Reminiscences: ....

....

....

....

....

....

Description: ....

Ring Gauge: ....

Draw: ....

Ash: ....

....

....

....

Price: ....

Affix label here

Brand: ....

Country: ....

Description: ....

Length: ....

Ring Gauge: ....

Strength: ....

Draw: ....

Burn: ....

Ash: ....

Flavor: ....

....

....

....

....

Personal Rating (1–10): ....

Venue: ....

Price: ....

Thoughts and Reminiscences:

....

....

....

....

....

....

Affix label here

....

Affix label here

Brand: ....

Country: ....

Length: ....

Strength: ....

Burn: ....

Flavor: ....

Description: ....

Ring Gauge: ....

Draw: ....

Ash: ....

....

....

Personal Rating (1–10): ....

Venue: ....

Price: ....

Thoughts and Reminiscences:

....

....

....

Warren Harding

Warren Harding owned and edited the Marion Star (Ohio) before entering politics in the early years of the twentieth century. His geniality and lack of pretension, combined with his reputation for enjoying late-night poker games and good cigars, endeared Harding to the common man. In 1920 he was elected the twenty-ninth president of the United States.

Brand:

Country: Description:

Length: Ring Gauge:

Strength: Draw:

Burn: Ash:

Flavor:

Personal Rating (1–10):

Venue: Price:

Thoughts and Reminiscences:

Affix label here

Affix label here

Brand:

Country:

Description:

Length:

Ring Gauge:

Strength:

Draw:

Burn:

Ash:

Flavor:

Personal Rating (1–10):

Venue:

Price:

Thoughts and Reminiscences:

Affix label here

Brand:

Country:

Length:

Strength:

Burn:

Flavor:

Description:

Ring Gauge:

Draw:

Ash:

Personal Rating (1–10):

Venue:

Price:

Thoughts and Reminiscences:

W. C. Fields

William Claude Dukenfield—W. C. Fields, for short—ran away from home at the age of 11 and by 14 had established himself as a professional juggler, even performing before Edward VII. In the 1930s and '40s he was a major Hollywood star, with films now considered popular classics such as My Little Chickadee *and* The Bank Dick. *A famous cigar smoker, Fields was quoted as saying, "I haven't been sick a day since I was a child. A steady diet of cigars and whiskey cured me."*

Brand:

Country: Description:

Length: Ring Gauge:

Strength: Draw:

Burn: Ash:

Flavor:

Personal Rating (1–10):

Venue: Price:

Thoughts and Reminiscences:

Affix label here

Brand:

Country: Description:

Length: Ring Gauge:

Strength: Draw:

Burn: Ash:

Flavor:

Personal Rating (1–10):

Venue: Price:

Thoughts and Reminiscences:

Affix label here

Affix label here

Brand:

Country: Description:

Length: Ring Gauge:

Strength: Draw:

Burn: Ash:

Flavor:

Personal Rating (1–10):

Venue: Price:

Thoughts and Reminiscences:

Clarence Darrow

Clarence Darrow gained early fame as a labor lawyer, defending the likes of Eugene V. Debs and labor leader William "Big Bull" Haywood. But it was his defense role in two of the most famous trials of the twentieth century—the Leopold and Loeb kidnapping and murder case, and the Scopes "Monkey Trial"—that the civil libertarian forged a national reputation. Darrow's success in court was the result of intense preparation, usually in the blue haze of cigar smoke, and masterly summations to juries.

Brand: ....

Country: .... Description: ....

Length: .... Ring Gauge: ....

Strength: .... Draw: ....

Burn: .... Ash: ....

Flavor: ....

....

....

Personal Rating (1–10): ....

Venue: .... Price: ....

Thoughts and Reminiscences: ....

....

....

....

....

....

Affix label here

Affix label here

Brand:

Country:

Length:

Strength:

Burn:

Flavor:

Personal Rating (1–10):

Venue:

Thoughts and Reminiscences:

Description:

Ring Gauge:

Draw:

Ash:

Price:

Affix label here

Brand:

Country:

Length:

Strength:

Burn:

Flavor:

Description:

Ring Gauge:

Draw:

Ash:

Personal Rating (1–10):

Venue:

Price:

Thoughts and Reminiscences:

George Sand

Wearing men's clothing and puffing proudly on small cigars, Sand was born Amandine Aurore Lucie Dupin in Paris in 1804 and came to international literary prominence for her masterpiece, History of My Life. *Franz Liszt introduced her to Frédéric Chopin, the great love of her life, whose career she nurtured and whose muse she inspired. Today there are George Sand Society cigar clubs in Santa Monica and New York City.*

Brand:

Country:

Length:

Strength:

Burn:

Flavor:

Personal Rating (1–10):

Venue:

Thoughts and Reminiscences:

Description:

Ring Gauge:

Draw:

Ash:

Price:

Affix label here

Brand: ....

Country: ....   Description: ....

Length: ....   Ring Gauge: ....

Strength: ....   Draw: ....

Burn: ....   Ash: ....

Flavor: ....

....

....

Personal Rating (1–10): ....

Venue: ....   Price: ....

Thoughts and Reminiscences: ....

....

....

....

....

....

....

Affix label here

Affix label here

Brand: ....

Country: ....

Length: ....

Strength: ....

Burn: ....

Flavor: ....

....

....

Personal Rating (1–10): ....

Venue: ....

Thoughts and Reminiscences: ....

....

....

Description: ....

Ring Gauge: ....

Draw: ....

Ash: ....

....

Price: ....

Rudyard Kipling

The author of such classics as Stalky and Co., The Jungle Book *and the poem* "If," *Kipling drew on his adventures in India and a vivid imagination. Short and slim, his most arresting features were bright blue eyes and heavy eyebrows, which shot up and down in time with the tip of his cigar as he talked. He won the Nobel Prize in Literature in 1907. Today, Rudyard Kipling is perhaps more famous for uttering the famous sexist remark, "A woman is just a woman, but a good cigar is a smoke."*

Brand: ....

Country: ....   Description: ....

Length: ....   Ring Gauge: ....

Strength: ....   Draw: ....

Burn: ....   Ash: ....

Flavor: ....

....

....

Personal Rating (1–10): ....

Venue: ....   Price: ....

Thoughts and Reminiscences: ....

....

....

....

....

....

Affix label here

Affix label here

Brand: ....

Country: ....

Description: ....

Length: ....

Ring Gauge: ....

Strength: ....

Draw: ....

Burn: ....

Ash: ....

Flavor: ....

....

....

....

Personal Rating (1–10): ....

Venue: ....

Price: ....

Thoughts and Reminiscences: ....

....

....

....

....

....

....

Affix label here

Brand:

Country:

Length:

Strength:

Burn:

Flavor:

Description:

Ring Gauge:

Draw:

Ash:

Personal Rating (1–10):

Venue:

Price:

Thoughts and Reminiscences:

Marlene Dietrich

Discovered by director Joseph Von Sternberg, Dietrich went from obscurity to the lead in The Blue Angel *in 1930 and soon achieved international fame. Taking up smoking in Berlin nightclubs in the '20s, she appeared as a cigar-smoking femme fatale in Orson Welles's* Touch of Evil. *If there ever was a woman who could make cigar smoking look positively feminine, it was Marlene Dietrich.*

Brand:

Country:

Length:

Strength:

Burn:

Flavor:

Description:

Ring Gauge:

Draw:

Ash:

Personal Rating (1–10):

Venue:

Price:

Thoughts and Reminiscences:

Affix label here

Brand: ....

Country: ....   Description: ....

Length: ....   Ring Gauge: ....

Strength: ....   Draw: ....

Burn: ....   Ash: ....

Flavor: ....

....

....

Personal Rating (1–10): ....

Venue: ....   Price: ....

Thoughts and Reminiscences: ....

....

....

....

....

....

Affix label here

Affix label here

Brand:

Country: Description:

Length: Ring Gauge:

Strength: Draw:

Burn: Ash:

Flavor:

Personal Rating (1–10):

Venue: Price:

Thoughts and Reminiscences:

Groucho Marx

Groucho, the most famous of the Marx Brothers comedy team, began smoking cigars at 15 while working vaudeville. According to his son, he picked up the fine habit from an old vaudevillian who had told him that a cigar was the most useful prop an actor could have onstage. "If you forget a line," Groucho once said, "all you have to do is stick the cigar in your mouth and puff on it until you can think of what you've forgotten." Groucho Marx favored Dunhill Havanas, particularly the 410, and also Belindas.

Brand: ....

Country: ....

Description: ....

Length: ....

Ring Gauge: ....

Strength: ....

Draw: ....

Burn: ....

Ash: ....

Flavor: ....

....

....

....

....

....

Personal Rating (1–10): ....

Venue: ....

Price: ....

Thoughts and Reminiscences: ....

....

....

....

....

....

....

....

Affix label here

Affix label here

Brand:

Country: Description:

Length: Ring Gauge:

Strength: Draw:

Burn: Ash:

Flavor:

Personal Rating (1–10):

Venue: Price:

Thoughts and Reminiscences:

Affix label here

Brand:

Country:

Length:

Strength:

Burn:

Flavor:

Description:

Ring Gauge:

Draw:

Ash:

Personal Rating (1–10):

Venue:

Price:

Thoughts and Reminiscences:

Jackie Gleason

Gleason entered show business through the cellar door as a carnival barker, master of ceremonies, disk jockey and occasional nightclub comedian. Following a lead role in the television show The Life of Riley *in 1949, he starred in* The Jackie Gleason Show *and* The Honeymooners, *a situation comedy in which he frequently smoked cigars. "The Great One," as Gleason came to be known, also earned critical acclaim for his acting in* Requiem for a Heavyweight *and in* The Hustler, *opposite Paul Newman.*

Brand: ....

Country: ....

Length: ....

Strength: ....

Burn: ....

Flavor: ....

....

....

Description: ....

Ring Gauge: ....

Draw: ....

Ash: ....

....

....

Personal Rating (1–10): ....

Venue: ....

Thoughts and Reminiscences: ....

Price: ....

....

....

....

....

....

....

Affix label here

Brand:

Country:

Length:

Strength:

Burn:

Flavor:

Description:

Ring Gauge:

Draw:

Ash:

Personal Rating (1–10):

Venue:

Price:

Thoughts and Reminiscences:

Affix label here

Affix label here

Brand:

Country: Description:

Length: Ring Gauge:

Strength: Draw:

Burn: Ash:

Flavor:

Personal Rating (1–10):

Venue: Price:

Thoughts and Reminiscences:

Greta Garbo

Greta Lovisa Gustafsson was discovered while working in a department store in Stockholm, Sweden. After a director changed her name to Garbo, she signed on with Metro-Goldwyn-Mayer in 1925 and went on to make twenty-four feature films, including classics such as Conquest *and* Ninotchka. *Her silky beauty, mysterious allure and reclusive life, in which cigars were some of her only companions, inspired a cult following.*

Brand: ....

Country: ....

Length: ....

Strength: ....

Burn: ....

Flavor: ....

....

Personal Rating (1–10): ....

Venue: ....

Thoughts and Reminiscences: ....

....

....

....

....

....

....

Description: ....

Ring Gauge: ....

Draw: ....

Ash: ....

....

....

....

Price: ....

Affix label here

Affix label here

Brand:
....

Country:
....

Length:
....

Strength:
....

Burn:
....

Flavor:
....
....

Description:
....

Ring Gauge:
....

Draw:
....

Ash:
....
....
....

Personal Rating (1–10):
....

Venue:
....

Price:
....

Thoughts and Reminiscences:
....
....
....
....
....
....
....
....

Affix label here

Brand:

Country: Description:

Length: Ring Gauge:

Strength: Draw:

Burn: Ash:

Flavor:

Personal Rating (1–10):

Venue: Price:

Thoughts and Reminiscences:

Alphonse Capone

The most notorious gangster in American crime history, Capone was born in Naples, Italy, but grew up in Brooklyn, where he joined the notorious Five Points gang. A razor slash to his face as a youth gave him the nickname "Scarface." Moving into Chicago, Capone and his henchmen dominated the city's bootlegging, gambling and prostitution for much of the 1920s. In 1931, after accumulating hundreds of millions of dollars, the cigar-chomping Capone was brought down on charges of income tax evasion and sentenced to Alcatraz.

Brand:
....

Country:
....

Length:
....

Strength:
....

Burn:
....

Flavor:
....

....

....

Personal Rating (1–10):
....

Venue:
....

Thoughts and Reminiscences:
....

....

....

....

....

....

Description:
....

Ring Gauge:
....

Draw:
....

Ash:
....

....

....

....

Price:
....

Affix label here

Brand: ....

Country: .... Description: ....

Length: .... Ring Gauge: ....

Strength: .... Draw: ....

Burn: .... Ash: ....

Flavor: ....

....

....

....

Personal Rating (1–10): ....

Venue: .... Price: ....

Thoughts and Reminiscences: ....

....

....

....

....

....

....

Affix label here

Affix label here

Brand:

Country:

Length:

Strength:

Burn:

Flavor:

Description:

Ring Gauge:

Draw:

Ash:

Personal Rating (1–10):

Venue:

Price:

Thoughts and Reminiscences:

Duke of Windsor

If Edward VIII was better known as the Duke of Windsor than as the King of England, it may be because he sat on the throne for less than a year. In 1936, Edward, the eldest son of George V, abdicated his title over opposition to his impending marriage to Wallis Simpson, an American commoner and divorcée. After that, he became the epitome of the English gentleman, wearing bespoke clothes and smoking cigars from Cuba, where he visited on numerous occasions.

Brand: ....

Country: .... Description: ....

Length: .... Ring Gauge: ....

Strength: .... Draw: ....

Burn: .... Ash: ....

Flavor: ....

....

....

Personal Rating (1–10): ....

Venue: .... Price: ....

Thoughts and Reminiscences: ....

....

....

....

....

....

....

Affix label here

Affix label here

Brand: ....

Country: ....

Length: ....

Strength: ....

Burn: ....

Flavor: ....

....

....

Personal Rating (1–10): ....

Venue: ....

Thoughts and Reminiscences: ....

....

....

....

....

....

....

Description: ....

Ring Gauge: ....

Draw: ....

Ash: ....

....

....

....

Price: ....

Affix label here

Brand:

Country:

Length:

Strength:

Burn:

Flavor:

Personal Rating (1–10):

Venue:

Thoughts and Reminiscences:

Description:

Ring Gauge:

Draw:

Ash:

Price:

Babe Ruth

George Herman Ruth, Jr., was arguably the best baseball player who ever lived, pitching over 29 consecutive scoreless innings in the 1916 World Series, batting .847 in 1920 and hitting 60 home runs in 1927. Known around the world as Babe and the Sultan of Swat, Ruth was also a world-class lover of beautiful women, good food, whiskey and Cuban cigars. He also owned part of the factory that produced five-cent Babe Ruth cigars.

Brand:

Country:

Length:

Strength:

Burn:

Flavor:

Personal Rating (1–10):

Venue:

Thoughts and Reminiscences:

Description:

Ring Gauge:

Draw:

Ash:

Price:

Affix label here

Brand:

Country:

Description:

Length:

Ring Gauge:

Strength:

Draw:

Burn:

Ash:

Flavor:

Personal Rating (1–10):

Venue:

Price:

Thoughts and Reminiscences:

Affix label here

Affix label here

Brand:

Country:

Length:

Strength:

Burn:

Flavor:

Description:

Ring Gauge:

Draw:

Ash:

Personal Rating (1–10):

Venue:

Price:

Thoughts and Reminiscences:

Edward VII

King of Great Britain from 1901 to 1910, Edward's behavior as Prince of Wales led to several social scandals but also to several No. 10 cigars named after him. Upon assuming the crown from his mother, Queen Victoria, who opposed smoking, Edward reportedly set all of England on a cigar-friendly course when he announced to the courtiers in Buckingham Palace, "Gentlemen, you may smoke."

Brand:
....

Country: .... Description: ....

Length: .... Ring Gauge: ....

Strength: .... Draw: ....

Burn: .... Ash: ....

Flavor: ....

....

....

Personal Rating (1–10): ....

Venue: .... Price: ....

Thoughts and Reminiscences: ....

....

....

....

....

....

Affix label here

Affix label here

Brand: ....

Country: ....

Length: ....

Strength: ....

Burn: ....

Flavor: ....

....

....

Personal Rating (1–10): ....

Venue: ....

Thoughts and Reminiscences: ....

....

....

....

....

....

....

Description: ....

Ring Gauge: ....

Draw: ....

Ash: ....

....

....

Price: ....

Notes

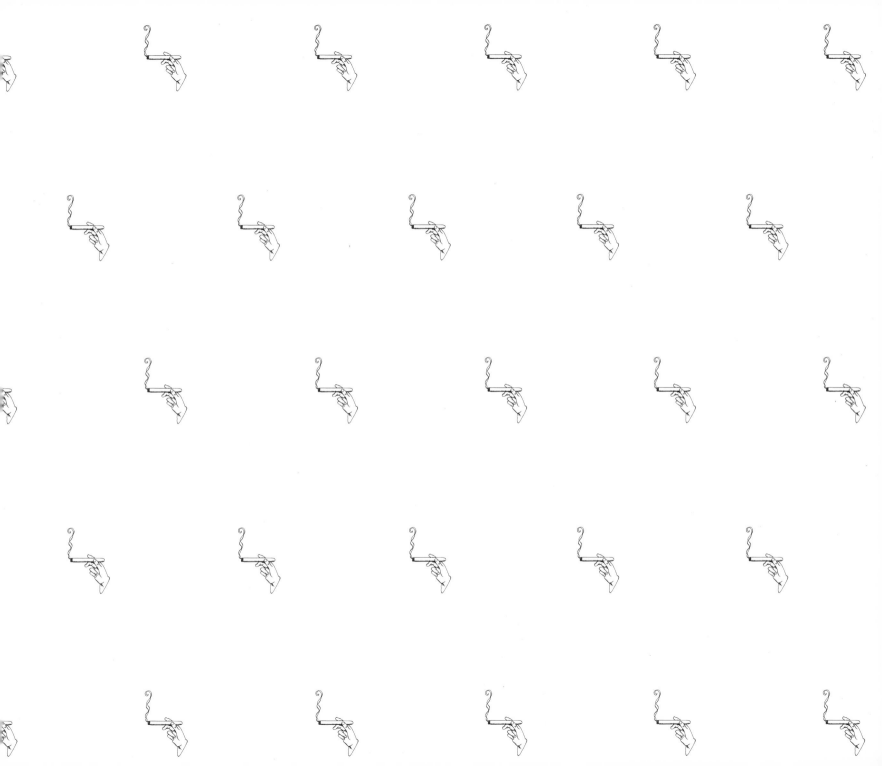